Reaganomics: Meaning, Means, and Ends

THE CHARLES C. MOSKOWITZ MEMORIAL
LECTURES

NUMBER XXIV

John Kenneth Galbraith

Paul M. Warburg Professor of
Economics Emeritus,
Harvard University

Paul W. McCracken

Edmund Ezra Day Distinguished University
Professor of Business Administration,
The University of Michigan, and
Chairman, Council of Economic
Advisers, American Institute for
Public Policy Research

Reaganomics: Meaning, Means, and Ends

The Charles C. Moskowitz Memorial Lectures
College of Business and Public Administration
New York University

THE FREE PRESS
A Division of Macmillan, Inc.
NEW YORK

Collier Macmillan Publishers
LONDON

24819591

Copyright © 1983 by New York University

THE FREE PRESS
A Division of Macmillan, Inc.
866 Third Avenue, New York, N.Y. 10022

Collier Macmillan Canada, Inc.

Printed in the United States of America

printing number

1 2 3 4 5 6 7 8 9 10

Library of Congress Cataloging in Publication Data

Galbraith, John Kenneth
  Reaganomics: meaning, means, and ends.

  (The Charles C. Moskowitz memorial lectures; no. 24)
    1. United States—Economic policy—1981-   —Address-
es; essays, lectures. 2. Supply-side economics—
Addresses, essays, lectures. I. McCracken, Paul Winston
          II. Title. III. Series.
  HC106.8.G34   1983   .   338.973   83-48640
  ISBN 0-02-922890-5

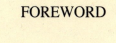

FOREWORD

This volume, the twenty-fourth in the Charles C. Moskowitz Memorial Lectures series (see p. 13), is concerned with the deeper implications of what has been loosely called "Reaganomics." It was not our intention here to review simply "supply-side" economics, or monetary and fiscal policies, or inflation and unemployment, or any of the other aspects of our economic condition which have already been so extensively discussed by so many with so little positive results. Instead, we invited our distinguished lecturers, Professors John Kenneth Galbraith and Paul W. McCracken, to focus on the Reagan Administration's avowed goal of altering fundamentally the relationship between government and society which had developed over the prior half century.

Professor Galbraith attacked the issue frontally, bringing together analytical threads developed over the years in such well-known works as *The Affluent Society, American Capitalism, The New Industrial*

State, and *Economics and the Public Purpose.*
Woven together, they appear somewhat as follows,
although excessively simplified and minus Professor
Galbraith's marvelous mastery of our language. Capitalism, despite the devoted defense of its devotees, is
defunct, because its central mechanism, the market,
no longer operates effectively to bring together pro-
ductive resources and transform them into goods and
services which, in aggregate, enhance public good.
But capitalism cannot be blamed for this failure, any
more than the noncapitalist countries can be blamed
for the failures of their systems, because all these
systems fail to confront and to come to grips with the
most basic and central reality of our time, i.e., the
triumph, omnipresence, and omniscience of large organizations and the bureaucracies which dominate
and direct them. Professor Galbraith, convinced that
his vision is clear in discerning reality, dubs our time
the Age of Organization, and, in the United States, he
identifies three great organizational loci of power—
the government, the corporation, and the trade union.
Each of them, it must be noted, operates so as to make
the marketplace no longer the central element in the
economy's decision-making mechanism. Of course,
as Professor Galbraith readily and even gleefully ad-
mits, "Many of my fellow economists do not
agree."

　　If one accepts that scenario, then what is to be
done? Professor Galbraith has a suggestion, which is
profoundly contrary to the Reagan Administration's
policy of reducing the role of government and, hopefully, reestablishing the ability of the market to function. He argues that that policy cannot succeed, for
the market requires active competition (i.e., rivalry
and adversarial relationships between and among

producers and consumers), while the great organizations do not respond according to that theory. Thus when monetary and/or fiscal policies seek to check inflation, they do so by putting pressure on the demand side of the market. But the dominant organizations do not respond by cutting wages and prices. Consequently, sales, production, and employment sag and the public suffers. Therefore, the thing to do is to accept the centrality of organizations and their power, and to work to build mechanisms for interorganizational negotiation and conciliation to replace the adversarial competition of the classical market. Also, since organizations are susceptible to senescence and an inherent tendency to become bloated bureaucracies, we should seek to bring younger men and women into positions of executive responsibility, hopefully so that their youth will prove invigorating and anti-atherosclerotic.

The foregoing seeks to summarize the thesis of Professor Galbraith's lecture. It does not seek to debate it, although there are many challengers of intellectual repute who respond to Professor Galbraith's disdain for their ideas with their own disdain for his. But one point seems clear. Professor Galbraith's challenges, whether right or wrong, have been stimulating to research and debate for at least three decades, and such research and debate can only contribute to greater insight and understanding in the long run.

Professor McCracken, not given to grandiloquent generalizations, approached assessing the Reagan Administration's policies in a more measured and conservative manner, noting that history's evaluation is likely to be quite different from the one arrived at in a contemporary context. Thus, "bad policies may in midstream look as if they are working out well, and good policies to reverse major imbalances may inherently lead us through an interlude of travail.'' To judge the Administration's policies, Professor McCracken felt it necessary first to describe the historical background. Having done so, he reviewed what he described as the five basic elements (or hypotheses) which underlay Reaganomics. With those analytical pieces in place, he arrived at his evaluation.

The historical backdrop shows an extraordinary two decades of economic growth and prosperity after World War II. This period was characterized by stable prices, low unemployment, and rapid growth in world trade and real incomes. Our performance deteriorated rapidly, however, in the seventies, and in the last couple of years gains virtually ceased. Inflation became pervasive, real income stagnated, and unemployment rose to levels unknown since the Great Depression of the thirties. Concurrently, world trade stagnated, and protectionist pressures built strongly everywhere.

While the causes could be found in such worldwide developments as the collapse of the Bretton Woods monetary system of fixed exchange rates, a period of worldwide crop shortages, and an explosion of energy prices, Professor McCracken observes that some countries handled these developments much better than others. In particular, West Germany, Japan, and Switzerland, all almost totally dependent on oil imports, suffered much less from inflation and adverse productivity developments than did the United States. The clear implication is that our problem was in our policies rather than in our luck.

Reaganomics sought to reverse the trend of the American economy in this context. It did so on the basis of five major assumptions: (1) inflation could be tamed without major adverse effects on employment, output, and real income; (2) a more stable management of monetary policy would be the key to a more stable economy; (3) a liberal international economic order is vital to the United States and the rest of the Free World; (4) tax-rate reductions would energize incentives, activate the economy, and produce larger tax revenues than otherwise; and (5) the scope of government, through direct regulation and fiscal operations, had grown excessively and should be contracted.

In sum, Professor McCracken's evaluation leads to a qualified passing grade, which probably ought to be, in academic parlance, an ''Incomplete.'' The major failures are in budget policies based on a highly questionable concept of supply-side economics, and in an abortive expectation that disinflation would not involve high unemployment. Massive tax cuts did put pressure on federal spending. But social expenditures could not be curbed enough to allow increased military spending and an approach to a balanced budget. There is future danger here. And inflationary expectations had become so deep-seated that prices could only be curbed by lost sales, and wages by lost jobs. However, there are major pluses: (1) the rate of increase in civilian government spending was slowed; (2) monetary policy is steadier and has overcome, at least for a while, the inflation monster; (3) some progress has been made in retarding the rate at which we were moving away from a liberal economic order; and (4) a basic shift toward improvements in productivity and labor cost per unit of output appears underway. On balance, it was vital that we overcome inflation.

The future will depend on whether we have won the war or only a battle.

These lectures present quite different views of the Reagan Administration and its policies. To Professor Galbraith, Reaganomics seems irrelevant because it fails to reckon with the underlying realities of the contemporary age, i.e., the dominance of organizational power centers over the market. To Professor McCracken, on the other hand, the market is real, and while its health may be somewhat impaired, it is still the central economic institution. Thus his evaluation of the Administration's policies is based on economic analysis and arrives at a qualified passing grade—at midterm. The final grade will not be in until the end of the "semester," or possibly later.

I express appreciation to Susan Landis for the editorial preparation of the volume and also to Susan and to Virginia Moress my appreciation for the handling of all the arrangements for the lectures. I also express my appreciation to Professors Ernest Bloch and Ernest Kurnow, who are the faculty members of the Charles C. Moskowitz Memorial Lecture Committee. I appreciate too the efficiency and care with which The Free Press handled the production of this small but significant volume.

Abraham L. Gitlow, Dean
College of Business and
Public Administration
New York University
February 4, 1983

THE CHARLES C. MOSKOWITZ
MEMORIAL LECTURES

THE CHARLES C. MOSKOWITZ MEMORI-
AL LECTURES were established through the gener-
osity of a distinguished alumnus of the College of
Business and Public Administration, the late Charles
C. Moskowitz of the Class of 1914.

It was Mr. Moskowitz's aim to contribute to the
understanding of functional issues of major concern
to business and the nation by providing a public for-
um for the dessemination of enlightened business the-
ories and practices.

A pioneer in the American motion-picture industry, Charles Moskowitz worked with other inno-
vators to create a business and entertainment phenomenon of enormous influence. He retired only
after many years as Vice-President and Treasurer,
and a Director, of Loew's, Inc.

This volume is the twenty-fourth in the Moskowitz series. The earlier ones are:

February, 1961	*Business Survival in the Sixties* *Thomas F. Patton,* President and Chief Executive Officer Republic Steel Corporation
November, 1961	*The Challenges Facing Management* *Don G. Mitchell,* President General Telephone and Electronics Corporation
November, 1962	*Competitive Private Enterprise Under Government Regulation* *Malcolm A. MacIntyre,* President Eastern Air Lines
November, 1963	*The Common Market: Friend or Competitor?* *Jesse W. Markham,* Professor of Economics, Princeton University *Charles E. Fiero,* Vice President, The Chase Manhattan Bank *Howard S. Piquet,* Senior Specialist in International Economics, Legislative Reference Service, The Library of Congress
November, 1964	*The Forces Influencing the American Economy* *Jules Backman,* Research Professor of Economics, New York University *Martin R. Gainsbrugh,* Chief Economist and Vice President, National Industrial Conference Board

15

November, 1965   *The American Market of the Future*
Arno H. Johnson, Vice President and Senior Economist, J. Walter Thompson Company
Gilbert E. Jones, President, IBM World Trade Corporation
Darrell B. Lucas, Professor of Marketing and Chairman of the Department, New York University

November, 1966   *Government Wage-Price Guideposts in the American Economy*
George Meany, President, American Federation of Labor and Congress of Industrial Organizations
Roger M. Blough, Chairman of the Board and Chief Executive Officer, United States Steel Corporation
Neil H. Jacoby, Dean, Graduate School of Business Administration, University of California at Los Angeles

November, 1967   *The Defense Sector in the American Economy*
Jacob J. Javits, United States Senator, New York
Charles J. Hitch, President, University of California
Arthur F. Burns, Chairman, Federal Reserver Board

November, 1968   *The Urban Environment: How It Can Be Improved*

William E. Zisch, Vice-chairman of the Board, Aerojet-General Corporation

Paul H. Douglas, Chairman, National Commission on Urban Problems

Professor of Economics, New School for Social Research

Robert C. Weaver, President, Bernard M. Baruch College of the City University of New York

Former Secretary of Housing and Urban Development

November, 1969   *Inflation: The Problem It Creates and the Policies It Requires*

Arthur M. Okun, Senior Fellow, The Brookings Institution

Henry H. Fowler, General Partner, Goldman, Sachs & Co.

Milton Gilbert, Economic Adviser, Bank for International Settlements

March, 1971   *The Economics of Pollution*

Kenneth E. Boulding, Professor of Economics, University of Colorado

Elvis J. Stahr, President, National Audubon Society

Solomon Fabricant, Professor of Economics, New York University

Former Director, National Bureau of Economic Research

Martin R. Gainsbrugh, Adjunct Professor of Economics, New York University

Chief Economicst, National Industrial
Conference Board

April, 1971   *Young America in the NOW World*
               Hubert H. Humphrey, Senator from
                  Minnesota
               Former Vice President of the United States

April, 1972   *Optimum Social Welfare and Productivi-*
               ty: A Comparative View
               Jan Tinbergen, Professor of Development
                  Planning, Netherlands School of Eco-
                  nomics, Nobel Laureate.
               Abram Bergson, George E. Baker Pro-
                  fessor   of   Economics,   Harvard
                  University
               Fritz Machlup, Professor of Economics,
                  New York University
               Oskar Morgenstern, Professor of Eco-
                  nomics, New York University

April, 1973   *Fiscal Responsibility: Tax Increases or*
               Spending Cuts?
               Paul McCracken, Edmund Ezra Day Uni-
                  versity, Professor of Business Admin-
                  istration, University of Michigan
               Murray L. Weidenbaum, Edward Mal-
                  linckrodt Distinguished University Pro-
                  fessor, Washington University
               Lawrence S. Ritter, Professor of Finance,
                  New York University
               Robert A. Kavesh, Professor of Finance,
                  New York University

March, 1974   *Wall Street in Transition: The Emerging System and its Impact on the Economy*

Henry G. Manne, Distinguished Professor of Law, Director of the Center for Studies in Law and Economics, University of Miami Law School

Ezra Solomon, Dean Witter Professor of Finance, Stanford University

March, 1975   *Leaders and Followers in an Age of Ambiguity*

George P. Schultz, Professor, Granduate School of Business, Stanford University

President, Bechtel Corporation

March, 1976   *The Economic System in an Age of Discontinuity: Long-Range Planning or Market Reliance?*

Wassily Leontief, Nobel Laureate, Professor of Economics, New York University

Herbert Stein, A. Willis Robertson Professor of Economics, University of Virginia

March, 1977   *Demographic Dynamics in America*

Wilber J. Cohen, Dean of the School of Education and Professor of Education and of Public Welfare Administration, University of Michigan

Charles F. Westhoff, Director of the Office of Population Research and

Maurice During Professor of Demographic Studies, Princeton University

March, 1978   *The Rediscovery of the Business Cycle*
Paul A. Volcker, President and Chief Executive Officer, Federal Reserve Bank of New York

March, 1979   *Economic Pressure and the Future of The Arts*
William Schuman, Composer
Roger L. Stevens, Chairman of the Board of Trustees, John F. Kennedy Center for the Performing Arts

April, 1980   *Presidential Promises and Performance*
McGeorge Bundy, Professor of History, Faculty of Arts and Science, New York University
Edmund S. Muskie, Former U.S. Senator from Maine, Secretary of State

March, 1981   *Econometric Models as Guides for Decision-Making*
Lawrence R. Klein, Benjamin Franklin Professor of Finance and Economics, University of Pennsylvania, Nobel Laureate

March, 1982   *The American Economy, 1960–2000*
Richard M. Cyert, President, Carnegie–Mellon University

20

Note: All but the last six volumes of The Charles C. Moskowitz
Memorial Lectures were published by New York University Press, 21 West Fourth Street, New York, N.Y.
10003. The 1977, 1978, 1979, 1980, 1981, and 1982
lectures were published by The Free Press.

CONTENTS

REAGANOMICS: A MIDTERM VIEW

John Kenneth Galbraith
Paul M. Warburg Professor
of Economics Emeritus
Harvard University

In one of the oldest and best-respected traditions of the public lecture, I begin with an irrefutable proposition. It is that capitalism, or what is still so denominated, is not working very well in the older industrial countries. Its poor performance in the United States, the United Kingdom, and, if in slightly lesser nature, Western Europe is having a blighting effect on economic progress—and solvency—around the world and notably in the states that emerged into independence in the years following World War II. It is not without interest or relevance that the economic performance in the socialist and Communist world is also far from favorable. I shall argue that the controlling economic development in our time is by no means confined to the nonsocialist countries. However, I shall be speaking in the main of the older western economies, especially those of the United States, Britain, and Western Europe. It is my purpose to go a bit behind the headlines to the deeper forces that shape the present and the future—and that are the basis of our present difficulties.

The controlling economic development in our time, a point I have urged in the past, is the rise of organization—the general movement, were one permitted to put matters in a slightly too dramatic form, from the age of capitalism to the age of organization. This is part of an historical process which, in principle, we accept; one does not earn a reputation for novelty by asserting that economic and social life is in a state of constant change. However, the change that we accept in principle we do not act on in practice. In consequence, we have not accommodated attitude, analysis, and policy to the economic, social, and political structures that now exist. Instead, and most notably in the United States and Britain, the political tendency has been to deny that there has been change. The approved policies are those appropriate to an earlier stage of market capitalism, a step backward celebrated by the phrase ''a return to fundamentals.'' These policies—the monetarist commitment in Britain and the monetarist and supply-side policies in the United States—have contributed in a substantial way to making the economic performance worse. But let me go back to the beginning: what is the evidence of the change that I am asserting? One is right to react suspiciously to anyone who speaks of great change in the social and economic fabric without illustration or proof. The process to which I advert today has the advantage of being visible to all who have the eyes and the will to see.

Organization, the subordination of the individual to the common purposes of a highly structured association, is a general phenomenon. For economic purposes, however, it has three relevant manifestations—in the modern corporation, the modern trade union, and the modern state. In all three of these, but especially in the corporation and the state, organization—bureaucracy—has become the decisive source of power and the controlling influence on economic behavior. What is still called the free enterprise system is, in practice, an array of massive organizational structures. This is most readily evident in the case of modern corporate enterprise.

A thousand or so large corporations now supply approximately two-thirds of the privately produced goods and services in the United States. This concentration is not, however, peculiar to any one country; there is similar concentration in all the other industrial lands; it is a basic imperative of the modern economic system.

With the rise of the great corporation goes a major shift in power to organization—to the corporate management. This is largely accepted, at least in practice. Few now seriously pretend that stockholders—the owners of the modern enterprise—are a significant force in its practical guidance. In the United States a banal annual ceremony, the stockholders' meeting, celebrates the irrelevance of the owners and ratifies for a largely honorific role the board of directors that the management has already selected. Authority not only rests with the organization—the bureaucracy—but, in substantial measure, it resides well within it. Except in the industry itself no one any longer knows the name of the head of a large American or British firm unless, perchance, that corporation is in serious trouble. Then the chief executive officer may command a certain attention for his explanations, for government help, or by being fired.

The role of organization—bureaucracy—in the modern state is not, of course, in dispute. It is a matter of everyday comment; all recent Presidents of the United States have reacted to its power. It was President Kennedy's delight, twenty years ago, to say, when presented with some plausible suggestion for a new course of public policy, "Well, I agree, but I don't think we can get the government to agree." What remains, as regards the great and massive structure of the modern state, is the impression, cultivated by the more ephemeral sort of politician, that somehow it can be made to disappear. It will not. None can doubt that there is a certain room for romance in all public discussion, but it should not be carried to extremes. Like the great corporation, the modern state with its massive bureaucracy is here to stay.

So is the trade union. It is an integral part of the contemporary industrial scene; there is today no industrial country where trade union organization has not reached a high level of development. In the United States there is an ebb-and-flow process in union power; of late, we have been on an ebb tide. But even where unions do not exist, the threat that there might be one is a powerful force in setting wages and benefits. So is the wages-and-benefits pattern that the unions establish for all workers. The great management-controlled corporation, the bureaucratically powerful state, and the trade union constitute the basic triad of modern economic society.

The primary effect of the rise of organization has been on the classical market—on both its operation and its ethic. The accepted purpose of the trade union is to replace the determination of wages *by* the market with a process of negotiation which protects the individual union member *from* the market. The great apparatus of the modern state has two broad functions. One is to render those services—provision of education, housing, health care, and the national defense—that do not come or do not come adequately from the market. The second function—as with farm-price supports, minimum-wage legislation, unemployment compensation, old-age pensions—is to temper the crude thrust of the market as it affects the particular individual or firm. Thus the state supplements, replaces, or modifies the working of the market.

Finally, it is one of the clear purposes of the modern great corporation to achieve a measure of control over the prices it pays and receives and over the response of consumers to those prices. The latter is what modern advertising and merchandising are all about.

Thus the age of organization, in all of its principal manifestations, has brought a displacement of the operation of the classical market. With this view, I am forced to concede, many of my fellow economists do not agree. No one familiar with my profession can doubt the ingenuity and determination with which numerous of its members divert their attention from what cannot readily be reconciled with their geometry, their algebra, or their preconception. However, reality does not yield to professional convenience.

The age of organization involves a massive assault on what may be called the ethic of the market economy and society. In the market economy adversary interests are arbitrated by the market. An adversary interest on wages between employer and employee is arbitrated by the market; an adversary interest on prices between raw-material supplier and manufacturer and between producer and consumer is also arbitrated by the market. And on market intervention and regulation there is a generally adversary relationship between the business firm and the state. It is taken for granted that taxation, regulation, and the extension of state activities into the private sector are to be resisted.

With the rise of organization, the ethic of negotiation replaces the adversary market arbitration. Or it should. Conciliation is the basis of successful association between organizations; the alternative is a mutually damaging conflict. There is strong resistance to this change; the notion of an inherently adversary relationship between business, labor, and government is very deep in the industrial psyche. We are only gradually coming to see that in those countries where the adversary relationship has been at least partly overcome—Japan being the most prominent example—capitalism works much better than in those where adversary attitudes are still assumed and, it may be added, considerably enjoyed. This is a matter to which I will return.

In all of the industrial countries we will live successfully in the age of great organization only as we better understand the internal character and dynamics of organization. And only as we accommodate to the interrelationships between organizations and the resulting dynamic and as we move from the adversary to the conciliatory ethic that the age of organization requires. Let me be specific.

As to the internal dynamic of organization, we must accept that corporations, as also public agencies and all other organizations, have a basic tendency to age and senescence. They are not, as we have been disposed in the past to believe, blessed with eternal youth. And we must counter this aging process much more successfully than we have hitherto. We shall have taken a very considerable step when we recognize that such an aging tendency exists. One of its manifestations is the different levels of corporate performance as between the younger industrial countries and the old. What is currently being attributed to Japaneses genius in organization is at least partly attributable to the less durable advantage of greater youth. And contending with Japan for industrial achievement, we notice, are the *yet younger* corporate enterprises of Taiwan, South Korea, Hong Kong, and Singapore.

It should be one part of the solution that men and women come into positions of major responsibility in the modern corporation at a much earlier age than at present—in their late thirties or early forties and not, as now, in the last years before retirement. This would contribute to longer-range planning; executives would have to live with their errors of commission and their even greater errors of omission. They would still be in office.

We must recognize that it is the tendency of all organization as it grows older to define excellence in personnel as whatever most resembles what is already there and wisdom in decision as what most resembles what is already being done. In consequence, all organization can have a self-perpetuating excellence. And equally, alas, it can have self-perpetuating mediocrity and obsolescence.

It must further be understood that all organization, all bureaucracy, has an internal dynamic of expansion—expansion in numbers of people. This has long been recognized as regards the public bureaucracy. None should doubt that it also powerfully characterizes the private corporation. Prestige in organization depends on the number of subordinates the individual has; there is a general and powerful impulse to enhance position and importance by adding more. Nothing so relieves the individual from the terrible burden of thought as more assistants to help with this ungrateful exercise. Thus the pressure for bureaucratic expansion.

Myron Gordon, a professor at the University of Toronto, has recently undertaken to measure the cost of the bureaucratic apparatus in American manufacturing. Between 1947 and 1977, the share of total revenue going to purchased materials decreased from 40.3 percent to 35.6 percent; the share going to labor decreased from 25.6 percent to 21.0 percent. The share of revenue going to profits and taxes also decreased. The share going to the corporate superstructure—the white-color and executive bureaucracy—increased from 14.6 percent to a massive 26.2 percent. Over these years, he concludes, "the rise in output due to increased productivity was more than absorbed by the disproportionate rise in the cost of obtaining that output," that rise being in the overhead or the bureaucratic establishment.

In these last months, under pressure of recession, American corporations have been shedding salaried and executive personnel. The number so dispensed with in the case of the largest corporations runs into the thousands. *Fortune* magazine in a recent issue studied the process, gave advice on how the shedding could best be accomplished, and called the article in question "The Executive Recession." The resulting streamlining has been thought greatly to strengthen the enterprises so engaged. The question that arises in a most compelling way is why were those people hired in the first place, what were they doing before? The answer is that many originally came to the organization not in response to need, but in response to the dynamic of bureaucratic growth.

We must also recognize that a related dynamic characterizes the corporate structure in general. The size of the organization is the ultimate source of prestige, the prime test of achievement in modern industry. An accepted order of social precedence in all industrial countries accords the front rank—the head of the table—to the executive of the largest corporation. In consequence, size has become a goal in itself in the age of organization. Profits are not unimportant, but to be big is better. In these last years in the United States we have been witnessing a great combination movement—what has been called the takeover frenzy. (Marx, if he is watching, is nodding his head in self-approval. It is a spectacular example of what he delineated as the process of capitalist concentration.) In this great thrust there has been little or no discussion as to whether the merged enterprises would be more profitable. Almost no one supposes that to be the aim. The aim is to be bigger; that is the goal of those initiating the takeovers. It is a striking illustration of the dynamic of organization. Were it so perceived, it might also be regarded with less equanimity. The prospect, if the aim to be bigger continues, is for yet greater corporate bureaucracies given to yet deeper bureaucratic stasis.

A sacred myth, devoutly observed, holds that a

total difference divides the world of capitalism from the world of socialism and Communism. They are two different systems; they have nothing in common. As we reflect on the entry of the industrial countries into the age of organization, we have a better if less dramatic view. Modern communism is also an exercise in massive organization. China, the Soviet Union, and the Eastern European states are also struggling with the unsolved problems of organization, including its ineluctable tendency to age and associated sclerosis. In a world where so many seek difference and conflict, it is mildly rewarding to find that there is some convergence even when it is on common misfortune. The competition between capitalism and socialism in the future will be, in no small part, a competition to see which can best deal with the still unsolved problems of pervasive organization.

I turn back to capitalism and to the external manifestations of the age of organization—to the problems inherent in the relationship between the great organizations.

These problems arising from the interrelationship of organizations are twofold. And while they have had devastating consequences, they are not matters of any great intellectual complexity. Organization has added a major new dimension to the task of macroeconomic management of the modern economy. And it has rendered obsolete and aggressively damaging the traditional instruments of such management.

Specifically, organization, as it has matured in the older industrial countries, has introduced an interacting dynamic as between incomes and prices. Organized workers press for higher wages; corporations, strong in their markets, accede and then raise their prices; the higher prices bring new demands for wage and income increases. This is the modern form of inflation. One has no great sense of novelty in speaking of this phenomenon; like the organization which is its source, it is for all to see. Again, only economists deeply conditioned in the mystique of the classical market are able to avert their eyes. It is a tribute to the success of such conditioning that some do succeed in doing so.

The consequence of great organization, as noted, is that it renders nugatory and in fact deeply damaging the traditional means for controlling inflation. These traditional means—monetary and fiscal policy—both work by repressing the demand for goods. Monetary policy works by repressing demand from the spending and respending of borrowed money through high interest rates and restricted credit. Fiscal policy works by repressing demand from the spending and respending from public borrowing. If demand is sufficiently curtailed, which has been the recent effect of severe monetary restriction in the United States and Britain, wage-price inflation can be tempered. But in the highly organized economy—the economy of strong corporations and strong unions— the first effect of such restraint on borrowing and investment is not on wages and prices; it is on sales and production. And on employment. Only as these are severely restricted is there an effect on wages and trade union bargaining and on prices. Putting the matter in plain language, traditional monetary policy controls inflation in the highly organized economy only as it produces a painful recession. And this is not a conclusion derived from any deep theoretical introspection. The United States and Britain are currently suffering severe recessions—high unemployment, low utilization of plant capacity, the highest rate of business failures since the Great Depression, especially serious depression in what are called the credit-sensitive industries. All of this is the direct consequence of a commitment to astringent monetarism in the age of organization.

The recession has been made worse in the United States by the association of a tight monetary policy with a relatively loose fiscal policy—what we may call the supply-side aberration. Loose fiscal policy puts an added burden on monetary policy, involves a greater competition for lonable funds, and leads to high interest rates. In all economic management higher taxes are to be preferred to higher interest rates. Monetary and fiscal policy are no longer sufficient tools of management in the age of organization. But for repressing demand, when that is required, fiscal policy is much to be preferred to monetary policy.

It is an extraordinary thing we have done in the United States in these last years. Conservatives are in positions of authority. One must suppose that they are generally in support of capitalism, and also their own pecuniary interest. But in the name of getting back to fundamentals, they have avowed and adopted policies deeply damaging to the reputation of the economic system and deeply inimical to the economic interest and well-being of their own supporters. Since the days of Marx it has been assumed by people of all political faiths that economic determinism—the accommodation of political decision to economic advantage—is the basic tendency of modern govern-

ment. We are now discovering that the government of
Mr. Reagan responds to a higher call. It is for ignor-
ing the present, retrieving the past, marching to the
drums of the monetarists regardless of the economic
and social cost and the cost to the reputation of the
economic system it avows.

In the industrial countries we can no longer control inflation by the designs—notably the monetary
policy—that, in however a theoretical way, were appropriate to the classical market economy. Professor
Friedman is not wrong; but he is right only for the last
century. The adversary arbitration of the market must
be replaced by conciliatory bargaining between the
relevant organizations. Macroeconomic policy must
involve an incomes-and-prices policy worked out between corporations, unions, and government. As
compared with an incomes-and-prices policy im-
posed as now by recession, this is in the interest of the
unions, the corporations, and the public at large.
There is no alternative. If capitalism or what is now
so designated is to work, this is essential.

There is room for national differences as to how
this interorganizational policy will be effected. In the
United States it will almost certainly require a formal
structure of restraints on the highly organized sector
of the economy. (Where small-scale enterprise and
the market still function, such a structure is, of
course, neither necessary nor relevant.) These restraints must be negotiated—must reflect the ethic of
organization and thus of conciliation. However, in
our case compliance cannot be left to the decision of
the individual firm or union; this has the effect of
rewarding those that do not conform. In other countries less formal methods of negotiation and concilia-

tion are possible. In the case of Austria, Germany, Switzerland, and Japan, they are already in an advanced stage of development. The requirement is, however, the same in all countries: the negotiating and conciliatory ethic of organization has to replace the adversary ethic of the market.

Such are the internal and external imperatives if capitalism is to survive in this age of organization: An understanding of and response to the aging tendencies of organization and its powerful dynamic of bureaucratic expansion. An understanding of and response to the external dynamic of interorganizational relations—of wages on prices and prices on wages—which is the modern cause of inflation. A respect for the negotiating ethic of the age of organization as distinct from the adversarial ethic of the age of the free market.

My onetime colleague at Harvard University, Joseph Schumpeter, thought well of the capitalist system, but he thought poorly of its chances of surviving its critics and its own misappreciation of its character. I do not consider myself wildly optimistic; these last years have shown, in the older industrial countries, a notable tendency to self-inflicted damage. If we do better in the future, it will not be because we have succeeded in recapturing the past, but because we have learned to come abreast of the present.

NOTE

1. *Journal of Post–Keynesian Economics* IV:4 (Summer 1982).

REAGANOMICS: A MIDTERM EXAMINATION

Paul W. McCracken
Edmund Ezra Day Distinguished University Professor of
Business Administration
The University of Michigan

Chairman
Council of Economic Advisers
The American Institute for Public Policy Research

It is a privilege to be a part of the Charles C. Moskowitz Memorial Lectures series. These lectures, and their wider audience through the books, "make a difference" in focusing national thinking about major issues of public policy. And it is an honor to participate this year with Professor Galbraith, a towering figure of the profession and the literary world. Through no particularly discretionary decision on the part of either one of us, we complement each other well—quite obviously operating at decidedly different levels. And we have even occasionally been on the same side of a policy issue. The imposition of price and wage controls in the early 1970s comes to mind here—he supporting it comfortably, and I uncomfortably.

Since this colloquy is being held during the longest recession in four decades, and the unemployment rate has replaced the rate of inflation in the double-digit gallery, many would suggest that the

Administration has already flunked the course. Indeed, there are those who would insist that last month the electorate did a quite effective job of assigning a midterm grade to Washington.

We would do well, however, to ponder the matter a bit further. The conceptual framework that would make sense for arriving at some sort of evaluation of how a government is doing in its management of economic policies is surprisingly difficult to articulate. Measuring the government's objectives for its program against other alternatives one would really prefer could better be done with a straightforward essay on some such topic as "The Proper Goals of National Economic Policy." Whether the policies are making good progress toward the goals supported by the citizenry itself would presumably be a useful analysis, and seemingly consonant with the democratic tradition, but it is not amiss to remind ourselves that "the people" have in history supported objectives and programs whose attainment was flatly contrary to a liberal political and economic order. It has often been pointed out, for example, that until toward the end of the 1930s Hitler would have won an open election in Germany. And for most of his career Napoleon undoubtedly had the support of the people.

A less subjective score or grade might be arrived at by evaluating an Administration's success in achieving the objectives which it had set out for itself. At least a government's programs ought to move the economy toward what government itself thought was proper. Even that, however, does not dispose of the grading problems. How things look today depends on policies, but it also depends on the situation inherited when the policies were deployed. And the nature of economic processes being what it is, bad policies may in midstream look as if they are working out well, and good policies to reverse major imbalances may inherently lead us through an interlude of travail.

For this specific subject there is a further problem. This is the era of "nomics." We have seen allusions to Carternomics, Trudeaunomics, ergonomics, as well as Reaganomics. Now "Reaganomics" has been used so much, and is sufficiently onomatopoetic, as to make its users assume that it has a quite definite meaning until we confront the question "How is the term to be defined?" Then we find that we have a term without an agreed-upon meaning. To invoke a phrase from D. H. Robertson, we have a grin without a cat.

Par for the Economic Course

That as the 1980s moved on stage some changes in economic policy seemed to be in order was clear enough. The world economy was not performing well, and in this deterioration the U.S. economy was participating fully. We gain some perspective on this poor performance if we think back to where we were as the decade of the 1970s was itself waiting in the wings. In January 1969, the then outgoing Administration's Council of Economic Advisers, in its own Annual Report, expressed a quite sanguine view of world prospects: "In the past two decades, enormous progress has been made in building a closely knit international economy. Remarkable growth in the volume of international commerce has gone hand in hand with sustained world prosperity; each has contributed to the other.''[1] Even after the normal discount applied to prose emanating from the political arena, most of us would agree that this statement reflected the prevailing view of that era. For two decades the U.S. economy had been performing not only well but better than its historical average (and its track record through history has in some important respects been better than our subjective image of it). Not only did the American resume its capability, after World War II, to deliver gains in real income and productivity but these gains were emerging at an accelerating pace. Real output per capita in the quarter of a century or so after World War II was rising at a 2.3 percent per year pace, a substantially stronger rate than in earlier periods. And gains in output per man-hour during this period at just over 3 percent per year were substantially higher than the 2 to 2.5 percent per year rate that had prevailed from the latter part of the nineteenth century to the middle of this century. (See Table 1.)

Table 1. Increase in Productivity of the U.S. Economy (Average annual changes)

Period	Real Product per Capita	Labor Productivity
1800–1855	1.1%	0.5%
1855–1890	1.6	1.1
1889–1919	2.1	2.0
1919–1948	1.8	2.4
1948–1973	2.3	3.1

Source: John W. Kendrick, ''Productivity Trends and the Recent Slowdown: Historical Perspective, Causal Factors, and Policy Options.'' In *Contemporary Economic Problems, 1979*, edited by William Fellner (Washington, D.C.: American Enterprise Institute for Public Policy Research, 1979), p. 22.

The price-level performance was equally good. Prices had shown some tendency to rise more rapidly in the mid-1950s, rising 3.5 percent from 1956 to 1957, but by mid-1958 the price level was again stabilized, an essential stability which then held for about seven years. For a decade beginning with 1958, in short, the rate of inflation remained below the modest 2 percent per year average that characterized the first two-thirds of this century. Thus the early 1960s, often cited as the glory years for economic policy, inherited a price level that had been stable for several years—a heritage that never received its full credit for the economic performance of the early 1960s. Even with the acceleration after 1965, the pace of inflation remained below 3 percent until 1968. (See Table 2.)

The unemployment rate did remain high by historical standards in the 1960s. During the first two-thirds of this century unemployment averaged 4.8 percent of the work force if we exclude the two major wars and the Great Depression. (This 4.8 percent is,

Table 2. Increase in Consumer Prices
(Average annual rate)

Period	Rate
1900–1967	2.1%
1900–1915	1.3
1922–1929	0.3
1948–1967	1.7
1958–1967	1.6

Source: *Historical Statistics of the United States, Colonial Times to 1970*, (U.S. Department of Commerce, 1975), pp. 210–211. Computed from the U.S. Bureau of Labor Statistics, Index of Consumer Prices for All Urban Consumers.

therefore, an average for forty-five years.) From 1958 to 1965 the unemployment rate was about a percentage point above this historical average. This was, however, considered to be a manageable and transient aberration, since for a decade prior to 1958 unemployment was, on the average, just over 4 percent of the labor force. (Indeed, that was presumably the basis for the fact that 4 percent came into the lexicon of economists as "full unemployment"—a par figure which might have been set closer to 5 percent if there had been more awareness of history.)

There, then, was the background for evaluating American economic prospects a decade ago. Gains in productivity and real income had been exceptionally rapid, rates of inflation were rising but still at levels to which we would now aspire for the 1980s, and the unemployment rate was only slightly above its historical par.

This strong economic performance was fully shared by others in the industrial world. Rates of inflation were low, and the low and nearly identical rates of inflation for the Federal Republic of Germany and the United States provided the world economy with twin anchors of stability. (See Table 3.) While in Japan consumer prices were rising at a comparatively rapid rate, that economy was only beginning to emerge as a major international force. Moreover, Japan at that time had a bifurcated price level, with wholesale prices during the decade of the 1960s rising somewhat over 1 percent per year.

In this expansionist environment world trade could readily flourish, and it did. For all of the major economies exports increased more rapidly than the volume of economic activity, a characteristic that we would expect to see in a well-functioning world eco-

Table 3. Increase in Real GNP and Consumer Prices, 1960–1970 (Average annual rise)

Country	Real GNP	Consumer Prices
Canada	5.2%	3.0%
France	5.6	4.0
Germany	4.7	2.6
Italy	6.5	3.9
Japan	11.2	5.7
U.K.	2.8	3.9
U.S.	3.9	2.7

Source: *International Financial Statistics Yearbook, 1981* (Washington, D.C.: International Monetary Fund), p. 00.

nomic order. (See Table 4.) The differential in these growth rates was negligible for Japan and small for the United States. This, however, reflected an explicit strategy for Japan. The growth rate for its domestic economy was geared to its foreign-exchange earnings, which determined the upper limits of permissible imports, which set the path along which the domestic economy could expand. And for the U.S. economy its substantially increased integration with

Table 4. Increase in GDP and Exports, 1960–1970 (Average annual rate)

Country	GDP	Exports
Canada	8.4%	12.0%
France	10.2	11.5
Germany	8.4	10.1
Italy	10.5	13.7
Japan	16.8	16.9
U.K.	7.2	8.0
U.S.	7.0	7.7

Source: *International Financial Statistics Yearbook, 1981* (Computed from data in current prices) (Washington, D.C.: International Monetary Fund), p. 00.

world trade was still ahead. Even so, world trade was
rising more rapidly than world output. Decisions,
therefore, about production capacity could be made
on a more efficient basis as markets beyond national
boundaries became increasingly available, the vari-
ety and quality of products within the reach of consumers were enriched, and price levels were sub-
jected to the added disciplines of more extensive
competition from external sources.

The Deterioration of Economic Performance

That during the last decade or so the economies
of the industrial world did not continue to move along
this course is clear enough. It is, of course, true that
the history of many eras has been written as if there
were an earlier golden age before some sort of fall—
including the Garden of Eden before that seductive
apple initiated so much trouble. And there were, as
we look back, omens of less happy days for the economy ahead. In the mid-1950s we had a warning that
the economy, if pushed too hard, could generate an
accelerating price level. The "full employment" balance of trade for the United States was deteriorating
after the mid-1960s. And in the 1960s, even before
the sharp rise in defense spending incident to the
Vietnam conflict, each succeeding year's rise in the
price level, though small, was a bit higher than that
for the prior year.

Even so, the record is, of course, clear that the
world's economic performance was decidedly less
impressive in the 1970s. At the beginning of the
1960s the Organization for Economic Cooperation
and Development set as a target for the decade then

ahead an average annual growth in output and real income of 4.1 percent per year for its member nations. From the beginning the actual performance was above this target, so in 1965 a new target of 4.6 percent per year was set, and it also was exceeded by a small margin.[2] With this favorable experience as a background, the OECD in 1969 set a goal of 5.1 percent for the 1970s. From the beginning, actual performance fell well below this targeted path. Indeed, the annual average rate of growth for real output for the years from 1970 to 1980, for the OECD economies as a whole, was 3.3 percent, and as the industrial world moved into the 1980s, these gains virtually ceased.[3]

Other measures of economic performance became equally unsatisfactory. Rates of inflation, even for nations with mature political and economic structures, rose to levels that only a few years earlier would have been thought highly improbable except under pressure from accelerating defense spending. (For all of these countries their proportion of output being allocated to making provisions for external security was declining during these years.) The average rate of inflation for the "Big Seven" of the industrial world reached 12.2 percent in 1980 and 10 percent in 1981. Moreover, the world had lost one of its twin anchors of stability, as the U.S. rate of inflation rose to 11.3 percent for 1979 and 13.5 percent in the following year. Fortunately the price-level performance of Japan and the Federal Republic of Germany, both by 1981 in the 5 to 6 percent zone, was much better, but double-digit rates of inflation in the economy whose currency remained the kingpin of the international monetary system were a major source of instability. (See Table 5.)

Table 5. Rise in Consumer Prices (Average annual rate)

Country	1961–70	1971–78	1979	1980	1981	1982*
Canada	2.7%	7.6%	9.1%	10.1%	12.5%	11.3%
France	4.0	9.0	10.8	13.6	13.4	13.9
Germany	2.7	5.2	4.1	5.5	5.9	5.0
Italy	3.9	13.0	14.8	21.2	19.5	15.8
Japan	5.8	9.8	3.6	8.0	4.9	2.8
United Kingdom	4.1	13.2	13.4	18.0	11.9	9.4
United States	2.8	6.7	11.3	13.5	10.4	6.6
Austria	3.6	6.6	3.7	6.4	6.8	5.8
Belgium	3.0	7.8	4.5	6.6	7.6	8.4
Denmark	5.9	9.6	9.6	12.3	11.7	10.0
Finland	5.0	11.6	7.5	11.6	12.0	9.6
Greece	2.1	12.4	19.0	24.9	24.5	21.8

Iceland	11.9	28.7	44.1	57.5	51.6	41.2
Ireland	4.8	13.2	13.3	18.2	20.4	18.9
Luxembourg	2.6	6.9	4.5	6.3	8.1	8.1
Netherlands	4.0	7.8	4.2	6.5	6.7	6.6
Norway	4.5	8.5	4.8	10.9	13.6	11.4
Portugal	3.9	18.2	23.9	16.6	20.0	26.0
Spain	6.0	15.2	15.7	15.5	14.6	14.0
Sweden	4.0	8.9	7.2	13.7	12.1	8.7
Switzerland	3.3	5.3	3.6	4.0	6.5	5.5
Turkey	5.9	24.1	63.5	94.3	37.6	39.8
Australia	2.5	10.6	9.1	10.2	9.7	10.5
New Zealand	3.8	11.8	13.8	17.1	15.4	15.8

*December 1981 to latest month, annualized.

Source: *Economic Outlook* (Paris: OECD, July 1982), p. 51.

World output and real incomes were also recording a poor performance. For the industrial world the gain in real output was 3.3 percent in 1979, 1.2 percent in 1980, less than 1 percent in 1981, and no gain at all in 1982. With such a sluggish pace of expansion on the part of these economies, unemployment rates increased sharply. Indeed, for the industrial world roughly 30 million people are now in the ranks of the unemployed. And the traditional tendency for unemployment rates elsewhere, particularly in Europe, to be substantially below those in the United States and Canada has faded, with unemployment rates in most of these economies now in or approaching the 10 percent zone.

World trade has also stagnated. Not only did the tendency for world trade to enlarge more rapidly than world output come to an end but the volume of trade itself reached a plateau in 1980, and the volume for 1981 was somewhat below that for the prior year (though world output rose slightly). These trends both reflected and accentuated the cumulating forces that have been pushing the world economy toward an illiberal international trading order.

Economic "Acts of God"

Now it is undeniable that the economic order has been buffeted during recent years by a congeries of *ad hoc* shocks—the economic counterpart of what lawyers call "acts of God." (Economists have been less imaginative about off-loading responsibility for our problems onto such unassailable shoulders.) There was, of course, the failure of the federal government to increase taxes in order to cover the increase in national security outlays incident to the Vietnam conflict—a fiscal failure so much discussed as to need no further belaboring. In passing, it is worth noting that the peak deficit during that period was $25.2 billion in fiscal year 1968. This was equal to 3 percent of GNP—above the average for the 1970s of just over 2 percent but well below this year's 5 percent.

The collapse of the Bretton Woods international monetary system of fixed exchange rates clearly imparted an inflationary bias to the management of monetary policies in the industrial countries. With exchange-rate movements, after the demise of fixed exchange rates, free to absorb the adjustments from swings in external trade, governments were seemingly liberated from the discipline of imposing restraint if their reserves of foreign exchange were being depleted. Exchange rates could simply adjust. The relaxation of monetary restraint throughout the industrial world was then dramatic. Rates of monetary expansion, as measured by the broadly defined money supply, briefly reached the 20 percent range even for the two anchors of stability in the industrial world (the Federal Republic of Germany and the United States) and 30 percent for Japan and the United Kingdom.[4]

In fact, the metamorphosis to a floating-rate system did not relieve countries from external disciplines, in the management of their domestic economic policies, to the extent that the theory of floating exchange rates seemed to imply. For one thing, in a floating system a deterioration in the exchange rate means *ipso facto,* and quite promptly, upward pressure on the domestic price level as import prices rise.

For countries whose external trade is large relative to the domestic economy, this adverse effect on the home price level can be substantial, and with the growing proportion of world output crossing national boundaries on its way to market, this effect could not be ignored even by the world's largest economies (including the United States).

Moreover, an important component of the old fixed-rate system remained—namely, that key currencies continued to play a significant role in world commerce. A large proportion of world trade was still denominated in dollars and sterling, and much of the borrowing and lending was in these major currencies. Thus governments continued to require reserves of foreign exchange, and in the management of their domestic economic policies what was happening to these reserves had to be taken into account.

For an interlude until these lessons were learned, however, the collapse of the old fixed-exchange-rate system did seem to impart an overly expansionist or inflationary bias to the management of domestic monetary policies.

At just this time some worldwide crop shortages occurred which exerted strong *ad hoc* upward pressures on price levels. For the United States producer prices of food stuffs and feed stuffs rose 58 percent from 1971 to 1973, and as these prices moved through the system, food prices confronting consumers rose sharply. Indeed, from 1972 to 1974 these prices, as measured in the consumer price index, rose 31 percent. Since food prices account for roughly 17 percent of consumer budgets, the direct effect on the price level was substantial. Moreover, the repercussion effects as these higher prices tripped off wage escalators, whose cost-raising effect produced price responses elsewhere, was large. And for economies with lower per capita incomes, where food constitutes a relatively larger proportion of total budgets, the resulting upward pressure on their general price levels was proportionally greater.

Finally, domestic price levels, and domestic economies generally, were thrown into disarray by the explosion in energy prices. The magnitude of this explosion is worth recalling again here. From 1972 to 1981 the index for prices of fuels, in the producer price index for crude materials, rose roughly five-fold, from 149 in 1972 to 752 in 1981, and the increase for prices at the consumer level rose from 120 to 407 during those years. (See Table 6.) Thus these items by the end of the decade cost 50 to 100 percent more, relative to the prices of things in general, than in 1973. Their "real" prices from 1972 to 1981 rose at the rate of 8.7 percent per year. The disequilibrating effects of these developments were large. They were another *ad hoc* thrust under domestic price levels forcing them upward, and again tripping off echo or repercussion effects on other costs and prices. They produced external payments imbalances forcing some nations into international borrowing to the point that they were mortgaging future export earnings—and laying the basis for future unease about the soundness of the international financial system. And it was leading some oil-exporting nations, benefiting from their newfound and seemingly unlimited cornucopia, to such an overvalued exchange rate that the industrial sector, whose development they hoped to finance with oil earnings, was not competitive in international commerce.

Table 6. Consumer and Producer Prices (1967 = 100)

	Prices of Fuels		Consumer Prices		Crude-Material Prices	
Year	Total Index	Index	"Real" a	Total	Fuel	"Real" b
(1)	(2)	(3)	(4)	(5)	(6)	(7)
1972	125.3	120.1	95.8	127.6	148.7	116.5
1973	133.1	128.4	96.5	174.0	164.5	94.5
1974	147.7	160.7	108.8	196.1	219.4	111.9
1975	161.2	183.4	114.0	196.9	271.5	137.9
1976	170.5	202.3	118.7	202.7	305.3	150.6
1977	181.5	228.6	126.0	209.2	372.1	177.9
1978	195.4	247.4	126.6	234.4	426.8	182.1
1979	217.4	286.4	131.7	274.3	507.6	185.1
1980	246.8	349.4	141.6	304.6	615.0	201.9
1981	272.4	407.0	149.4	329.1	751.5	228.4

aColumn 3 divided by column 2.
bColumn 6 divided by column 5.
Source: *Economic Report of the President*, Feb. 1983, pp. 222–8.

58

Clearly the fates seemed to hold a grudge against
the era that was to be the backdrop for the 1980s. That
our own economy and the international economic
order generally would be off balance from this series
of blows, most not primarily with an economic origin
but having large economic effects, seems reasonable
enough. Yet as we examine the evidence, we find
ourselves moving uncomfortably to the conclusion
that nations and governments were not just helpless
ships adrift on an angry sea. The record is not uni-
formly poor, suggesting that some were navigating
much better than others.

For the industrial countries as a whole, consumer prices rose 11.9 percent in 1980 and 10.0 percent in 1981. In 1980, however, the rise was as much
as 18 percent for the United Kingdom, 13.7 percent
for Sweden, and 13.5 percent for the United States,
but the figures were 5.5 percent for the Federal Republic of Germany, 8 percent for Japan, and 4.1 percent for Switzerland—most of these being countries
which must meet virtually all of their energy requirements from imports. (We see, of course, the same
divergence in Latin America, where in 1980 Argen-
tina's price level doubled and Brazil's rose 83 percent, but the figures for Ecuador and Guatemala were
13 percent and 11 percent respectively.)[5] For the
United States, labor costs per unit of output in 1981
rose substantially more than the annual average during the 1970s, but for Japan, the Federal Republic of
Germany, and the United Kingdom the 1981 rise was
less than in the prior decade. (See Table 7.) While all
countries have been experiencing reduced gains in
productivity, by the turn of the decade the figure for
the United States was the lowest of the Big Seven,

Table 7. Unit Labor Costs In Manufacturing (Annual rate of increase)

Country	1970–1980	1981
Canada	7.4%	10.0%
France	9.5	14.3
Germany	5.2	4.2
Italy	14.4	21.0
Japan	6.9	3.7
U.K.	14.2	8.7
U.S.	5.7	8.2
Total	7.5	8.5

Source: *Economic Outlook,* Paris: OECD, July 1982, p. 47.

and by some measures output per man-hour was declining. Indeed, earnings from an hour of work in the United States this year will buy about 6 percent less than five years ago. (Apart from transient wobbles in the data, gains in productivity and improvements in real income are alternative aspects of the same process.)

There, then, was the performance of the American economy as this decade opened. The low rates of inflation that had characterized the American economy during most of its history had given way to rates that would double the price level about every six years, and the pace was itself accelerating. The economy's capability historically for doubling material levels of living every generation, through its 2.5 percent per year improvements in productivity, had metamorphosed into a performance that delivered declining real incomes. While shocks, economic "acts of God," played a role in this deteriorating performance, nations which might have been expected to be more adversely affected turned in a better performance than the United States. The evidence was strongly suggesting that the problem was not our luck so much as our policies. And the outcomes of the elections in November 1980 suggested that the American people were ready for the exercise of their democratic right to turn the rascals out and let some new ones (carefully phrased to preserve some semblance of nonpartisanship) try their thing.

The Building Blocks of Reaganomics

What were the basic elements of the strategy for economic policy deployed by the incoming Administration at the beginning of 1981? While those in or close to the Administration in the early stages of framing its program might not agree precisely with this formulation, there seemed to be about five basic building blocks in this new strategy. First, the high and even accelerating rate of inflation could be brought down to more traditional levels (to, say, the 2 percent per year annual average that prevailed from 1900 to 1967) with small adverse effects on employment, output, and real income. Second, the key to a more stable economy is a more stable management of monetary policy. Third, a liberal international economic order is urgently important for the United States and the rest of the Free World. Fourth, a reduction in tax rates would so energize incentives and activate the economy that the lower rates would also produce even larger revenues than would otherwise occur. And, finally, the scope of government, both through direct regulation and through its fiscal operations, had expanded too rapidly. Suppose that we examine briefly each of these in turn.

Building Block I

What was the theoretical underpinning for the Administration's optimism about taming inflation without seriously adverse effects on the level of economic activity in real terms? This had a more solid foundation than some sort of vacuous hope that all would work out for the best in the best of all possible worlds. The concept of the natural rate of unemployment plays a role in this theory of inflation. It is a concept in some ways reminiscent of Wicksell's "natural rate" of interest in that its magnitude tends to be determined by "real" as opposed to nominal or monetary factors responsive to demand management policies. Milton Friedman is generally credited with this concept, though, as is true for most such items in our intellectual inventory, its roots extend back into earlier history.[6] According to the short definition, the natural rate of unemployment is the rate that would prevail if the expected rate of inflation were equal to the actual rate. There would then be no stimulus to employment and real output because of responses to demand management policies based on expectations that prices and wages would be lower than would turn out to be the case.

Friedman defines the natural rate of unemployment more precisely as "the level that would be ground out by the Walrasian system of general equilibrium equations, provided there is imbedded in them the actual structural characteristics of the labor and commodity markets, including market imperfections, stochastic variability in demands and supplies, the cost of gathering information about job vacancies, and so on."[7]

This does not, of course, imply some sort of iron law of unemployment, with the rate of unemployment forever being written in the stars. This rate, for example, could be reduced if such market imperfections as high minimum wage rates or mismatches between skill supplies and market requirements were moderated. What this does say is that expansive demand management policies will drive the actual unemployment rate below the natural level only by producing a higher rate of inflation than is then expected. People, however, learn. They begin to factor into their decisions and commitments the assumption of a higher rate of inflation. Then expansive demand management policies that produce another rise in the price level equal to the last one do not produce more output and employment. They produce only more inflation. And, indeed, there is no reason why consumers and businesses would not begin to factor into their expectations accelerating rates of inflation. Then even inflation at a rising rate, if expected, would not drive unemployment below its natural rate.

And this leads us to the theoretical rationale for optimism that the rate of inflation could be wound down with minimum trauma. If because of new policies people (businesses, consumers, and employees) expect that rates of inflation will now be lower, disinflationary demand management policies will be associated primarily with a lower pace of inflation rather than reduced output and employment. It would not, after all, be rational for businesses, consumers, and employees to base their actions on assumptions inconsistent with their expectations about the state of the economy within which these plans would be carried out.[8] A company making its own price decisions as if rates of inflation in the period ahead would be higher than the company itself expected would court the risk of lost sales. And unions that demanded wage adjustments consistent with rates of inflation higher then their own expectations would be embarking on a deliberate strategy to increase unemployment among its own members. Given these expectations, such actions would be "irrational."

The rising trend in the rate of inflation from, say, 1965's pace of just under 2 percent to the 6 percent zone during 1969 was accompanied by a drop in the unemployment rate from 4.5 percent in the earlier year to 3.5 percent in 1969. (See Table 8.) Demand management policies that were exerting strong upward pressure on the economy did drive the unemployment rate below the 4 percent that had come to be the calibration of full employment (and certainly below the 5 percent which was probably closer to the natural rate). This, however, was against the backdrop of a decade, beginning in 1958, during which the price level was essentially stable. A decade later, during the second half of the 1970s, the favorable effects on unemployment from policies that exerted inflationary pressure on the economy did not materialize. The rate of inflation rose steadily from 4.8 percent during 1976 to 13 percent for 1979 and 12.4 percent for 1980, but unemployment in 1980 was 7.1 percent, and for the lowest year (1979) it was still 5.8 percent. Even with demand management policies exerting enough pressure on the economy to give us, by the latter part of the 1970s, rates of inflation out of context with our history, the unemployment rate held in the 7 percent zone (about the same as in the recession years of 1958 and 1961). These

**Table 8. The Rise in Consumer Prices and the
Unemployment Rate**

Year	Rise in CPI[a]	Unemployment Rate
1955	0.4%	4.4%
1956	2.9	4.1
1957	3.0	4.3
1958	1.8	6.8
1959	1.5	5.5
1960	1.5	5.5
1961	0.7	6.7
1962	1.2	5.5
1963	1.6	5.7
1964	1.2	5.2
1965	1.9	4.5
1966	3.4	3.8
1967	3.0	3.8
1968	4.7	3.6
1969	6.1	3.5
1970	5.5	4.9
1971	3.4	5.9
1972	3.4	5.6
1973	3.4	4.9
1974	12.2	5.6
1975	7.0	8.5
1976	4.8	7.7
1977	6.8	7.1
1978	9.0	6.1
1979	13.0	5.8
1980	12.4	7.1
1981	8.9	7.6

[a]December to December.

Source: Data from *Economic Report of the President* (Washington, D.C.: U.S. Government Printing Office, February 1982), pp. 266, 295.

data are at least consistent with the hypothesis that businesses, consumers, and employees, having been burned by only slowly adjusting their expectations, formed initially during almost a decade of stability

beginning with 1958, did then finally adjust these
expectations to the new realities. And getting more
output and lower rates of unemployment by being
willing to accept yet a little more inflation was then
no longer an available option.

People had learned.

It is clear that the then new Administration in
early 1981 was counting heavily on this process to
work during the deceleration of inflation. If inflationary demand management policies led simply to more
inflation, as people learned and adjusted their expectations, was it not reasonable to expect disinflationary policies to produce reduced rates of inflation,
with also minimal effects on employment, output,
and real incomes? "Central to the new policy," said
the Administration in February 1981, "is the view
that expectations play an important role in determin-
ing economic activity, inflation, and interest rates."[9]

In some respects, some to be examined later,
this theory of policy seemed to work in practice. The
rate of inflation not only responded but the magnitude
of the response was much larger than most analysts,
inside the Administration and outside, had expected.
The rate of inflation during the year (December to
December) dropped from 12.4 percent during 1980 to
8.9 percent for 1981, and to somewhat over 6 percent
for 1982. This was a more rapid deceleration of the
inflation than even the new Administration was pro-
jecting—projections which seemed optimistic to
forecasters more generally. In February 1981, the
month the Administration issued its basic white paper, the monthly *Blue Chip Economic Indicators* report indicated a "consensus" projection of a 9.7 percent average rise in consumer prices from 1981 to

1982, and projections of the five econometric services cited in this report ranged from 8.9 percent to 10 percent. [10]

Reality started to diverge from expectations, however, with movements in output and employment. The February White House paper projected for the then following year (i.e., 1982) a gain in real output of 4.2 percent, and an unemployment rate of 7.2 percent. The actual figures will turn out to be something like −1.5 percent and 9.5 percent respectively. (See Table 9.) While the rate of inflation was reduced, the comparatively smooth winding down with minimal effects on output and employment did not occur.

Why did businesses and unions apparently not act rationally and scale down their price increases and wage demands, having been told what the economics game plan was to be? There were, of course, two sets of reasons. One has to do with institutional viscosities in our economic processes. Multiyear labor contracts will carry wage increases to the end even if disinflationary economic policies are deployed. Some incomes are adjusted upward on the basis of the rise in the price level in the prior period, even the prior year. Price escalators pertain to far more than wages in the modern economy. Even where formal price escalators do not prevail, after a long period of inflation income earners become accustomed to expecting what has become a conventional or "normal" magnitude of upward adjustments in wages and salaries—something like, say, 9 percent. With disinflationary policies being pursued, these momentum forces alone will tend to cause real labor costs to overshoot, producing a rise in unemployment.

Table 9. Percent Change In Consumer Prices, Output, and Employment

Year	CPI Actual	CPI Projected	Real GNP Actual	Real GNP Projected	Unemployment Rate Actual	Unemployment Rate Projected
1981	10.4%	11.1%	1.9	1.1%	7.6	7.8%
1982	6.5	8.3	-1.5	4.2	9.5	7.2
1983		6.2		5.0		6.6

Source: For 1981 and 1982 actual data: *Economic Indicators*, June 1983, pp. 2, 12, 23. Projected data are from *America's New Beginning: A Program for Economic Recovery* (White House, February 1981), p. 25.

The main source of this collision between disinflationary policies and wage and price decisions that theoretically would be rational only with a continuation of inflationary policies was quite simply that the disinflationary program was not expected to persist. For fifteen years Administrations of both political parties had assured the nation that inflation was bad and that policies would be deployed to counter it. There was the 1966 Federal Reserve crunch, the belated 1968 increase in taxes, the 1969–1970 disinflationary program, the 1974–1975 effort (which did bring the rate of inflation to the 5 percent zone by the end of 1976), and the various "guidance efforts" through the Council on Wage and Price Stability in the latter half of the 1970s. The 1966 monetary restraint was followed by much easier policies in 1967. Following the 1968 tax increase Washington became terrified at the thought that they might thus have been guilty of overkill, and the monetary faucets were opened up. (During the last half of 1968 M_1 and M_2 were allowed to expand at an 8 to 9 percent per year rate, an aggressive rate of monetary expansion for that period.) The disinflationary program of 1969 and 1970 had halted and then reversed the accelerating rate of inflation, bringing the rise in the price level below a 4 percent annual rate by the first half of 1971 (well below the 6 percent zone that had been reached by 1969 and early 1970). The tidal wave of support for price and wage control, heavily generated by the business community itself, swamped this effort by 1971. And the 5 percent rate of inflation closing out 1976 metamorphosed into the double-digit range as the 1980s opened (only a small part of which, as pointed out earlier, was really accounted for by shocks).

With this record for more than a decade of a large and growing gap between what government said and what it delivered, it was only reasonable to assume that an announcement by yet another Administration that it was going to deal with inflation was not apt to send businesses and unions scurrying to reformulate their wage and price strategies. "Wolf" had been called too many times. (Of course, finally there was a wolf.) A squeeze between a private sector which placed little credence in assertions that the price-cost level would be stabilized and disinflationary policies that this time did persist became inevitable. And this, together with the institutional momentum factor, inexorably led the economy into an interlude of slack and higher unemployment.

This does not, however, prove that the Administration's strategy was wrong.

Indeed, it is an accurate rationale of why an overly expansionist policy, which earlier did produce near-term gains in output and employment, finally brought the economy to high rates of both inflation and unemployment. The Administration did, however, misjudge the extent to which there would still be an interlude of "overshooting." Momentum factors and the understandable assumption that once again "Washington" would not persevere made it certain that there would be an interlude of slack in the economy on the way to a greater stability of costs and prices. The problem here was less an error of diagnosis than that some blood, toil, tears, and sweat rhetoric would have been in order. (In its Annual Report, February 1982, the Council of Economic Advisers did warn that there would be short-run costs before long-run benefits emerged.)

Building Block II

The Administration also made it clear from the outset that it considered a steadier and more moderate rate of monetary expansion to be an integral part of the forthcoming strategy for economic policy. "A stable monetary policy, gradually slowing growth rates of money and credit along a preannounced and predictable path, will lead to reductions in inflation."[11] Emphasis on the important role of money and the management of monetary policy was not, of course, unique to this Administration. Thinking had already come a long way from three or four decades earlier. The Economic Report of the President transmitted to the Congress in January 1950, for example, consists of seventeen pages, eight sentences of which allude dutifully to "credit policies." In both the scholarly world and in the arenas within which managers of economic policy operate internationally, the role of money and the management of monetary policies have been the recipient of persistently growing emphasis. This is epitomized by the contrast between the Economic Report of January 1950, with its brief bow toward credit policies, and the Economic Report for this year, in which the Council of Economic Advisers required a separate chapter of thirty pages to discuss "Monetary Policy, Inflation, and Employment," in which the Council declares: "The appropriate policy for reducing the inflation rate is a decrease in the rate of money growth. . . . If the decrease is generally anticipated, wages and prices will begin to rise more slowly and the adverse short-run effects on output and employment will be minimized."[12]

That monetary developments earlier had made their full contribution to our economic disequilibrium seemed clear enough. There were, in fact, two general problems with monetary policy during the 1970s. On balance it was too expansive. In half of the years during the decade the monetary aggregate, M_2, rose at double-digit rates. (See Table 10.) The 12.5 percent average rate during the three years ending with 1977, for example, certainly contributed to the high rate of inflation reached by the end of the decade.

While there is not a precise relationship between movements in M_2 and changes in the dollar volume of business activity, the economy has tended to move along the trail blazed by increases in the money supply. The increase from 1974 to 1977 in the money

Table 10. Increase in the Money Supply (December–December increase in M_2)

Year	Percent
1969	3.8%
1970	6.4
1971	13.5
1972	13.0
1973	7.0
1974	5.6
1975	12.7
1976	14.1
1977	10.8
1978	8.2
1979	8.2
1980	9.0
1981	10.1
1982	10.0

Source: Basic data from the Federal Reserve System. Mimeographed releases of March and June 1982; *Economic Indicators*, June, 1983, p. 26.

supply of 39.5 percent at least made possible the 33.7 percent rise in nominal GNP, and some would assert an even stronger causal relationship.

Moreover, monetary policy during this period had been managed in ways that produced an undesirably erratic course for the money supply. To some extent this is evident in the annual data. A 6.4 percent increase during 1970 was followed by 13.5 percent for 1971. The rise during 1974 was 5.6 percent, followed the next year by 12.7 percent, and over 14 percent in 1976.

This problem of erratic movements was particularly troublesome in 1980. During the first third of the year the money supply (M_2) grew at a 4.9 percent per year rate. For the next six months the pace jumped to a 14.2 percent rate, and then was sharply restrained at the end of the year.

Some new and quite fundamental analytical problems have, however, now begun to emerge. For one thing, major problems have emerged with the theory of money and monetary policy. As indicated earlier, money and monetary policy during the quarter of a century or so following World War II were finally rescued from the oblivion to which they had been relegated by the Keynesian revolution and the triumph of fiscal policy. The relationship between the quantity of money and the level of economic activity was finally once again seen as a fit subject for something other than musty discussions pertaining to the history of economic thought—even as a fit subject for analyses of current economic policy problems. The reason was quite simply that these relationships (between changes in the quantity of money and changes in the volume of business activity) seemed to be among the more stable patterns of regularity in economic life. A presidential address to the American Economic Association at the end of 1967 with the straightforward title ''The Role of Monetary Policy'' was still a bit startling, but a decade earlier it would have been greated with bemused incredulity. And after the usual lag between developments in the intellectual arena and their translation into the management of policy, central banks began to set objectives or targets for the growth in the money supply (a process in which the Deutsche Bundesbank played a leadership role).

At the time central banks began to draw upon these relationships between money and economic activity in the management of their policies, however, the relationships themselves began to display less regularity. And in recent years a large literature has developed on what economists call the stability of the demand function for money and what seems now to be creating instability in these relationships. This is not the place to review these research efforts, but one or two quick comments may be in order here. One possibility for increased instability in the relationship between the trail blazed by the rates of growth in the money supply and the path the economy follows along is the dynamic nature of innovation in financial markets and financial institutions during recent years. There was a time when checking was done against demand deposits at commercial banks, and there were definitive boundary lines between these funds and savings and time deposits, and between these deposits and other assets. Now M_1 must include not only currency and demand deposits but such other items as NOW accounts, automatic transfer service accounts, credit union share draft accounts, and still some others. And M_2 now embraces, in addition to M_1 plus savings and (small) time deposits, overnight RPs, mutual money market funds balances, and still some others. Since "the money supply" has become a less discrete entity, with the synergetic combination of deregulation and innovation enabling new assets to perform money functions, the amount of money required for any given level of business activity has become less certain.[13]

The instability may, of course, have had its origin in the growing uncertainties about the economy and the tendency, therefore, to hold more assets in cash. In that case a monetary policy permitting the money supply to increase along a previously decreed path would produce monetary dehydration. There is some evidence that this became a problem in 1982.[14]

Whatever the sources of this instability in the relationship between the level of business activity and the amount of their assets people want to hold in the form of money, and a good deal of uncertainty about it does remain, it has been a major limitation to any straightforward application of the quantity theory of money to the on-going management of economic policy.

Moreover, those in the Administration for whom monetary policy was the major instrument for influencing the course of the economy ran into an institutional problem. The Administration does not manage monetary policy. This is embedded in the Constitution itself. Item 5 of Article I, Section 8, outlining the powers of the Congress, gives that body the authority to "coin money, regulate the value thereof. . . ." The Federal Reserve System is then the agent of the Congress formed to carry out this responsibility. That this is all not a mere formality is indicated by the fact that the System's annual report is made not to the President but to the Speaker of the House of Representatives.

Moreover, accumulated experience internationally has led to the conclusion—indeed, tradition—that things work out better if the central bank is insulated from the sudden gales that from time to time roar through the political arena. It is often true that central banks are performing their most important role when they are least popular. What stability there has been in Italian economic policy, for example, has come primarily from the Bank of Italy. And the substantial *de facto* independence of the Deutsche Bundesbank enabled it to deploy policies that played an important role in that nation's Wunderwirtschaft after World War II.

Now this has never meant that the Administration must not consult with the Federal Reserve or make known its views. From time to time the President and the Chairman will consult. There must be regular consultation between the Treasury and the Federal Reserve. The three members of the Council of Economic Advisers have traditionally met periodically with the Federal Reserve Board. There is no shortage of opportunity for Administration officials to make known their views to the occupants of that marble palace on Constitution Avenue.

Overt, open pressures from Administration officials on the Federal Reserve, however, were something different. They collided with the long tradition pertaining to central bank "independence." And at a time when financial markets were already uneasy and off balance, these open arguments became an additional source of disturbance.

On balance, however, pressures for a steadier course of monetary policies were constructive. An unsteady path of expansion for the monetary aggregates had made the economy pursue an unnecessarily erratic course in the late 1970s and 1980, and the Federal Reserve profited (distasteful as it may have been) from these Administration pressures to try harder.

Building Block III

The international dimension of the Administration's economic program, when the new officialdom took over in January 1981, was clearly less defined than its views about domestic economic policy. The February 1981 *America's New Beginning: A Program for Economic Recovery,* for example, contains little about that subject. And it became clear early that the State Department was not well organized at the top to provide vigorous and coherent leadership for external economic policy.

A concatenation of developments was, however, destined to force more attention to these matters. For one thing, our external transactions had become much more important in understanding domestic economic developments. By the beginning of the 1980s almost one-fifth of the ''goods output'' (GNP less construction and services) of the American economy was crossing a national boundary on its way to market, a proportion that had somewhat more than doubled from 1970 to 1980. (See Table 11.) Nor was this

**Table 11. U.S. Merchandise Exports and Goods GNP
(Dollar amounts in billions)**

| | | Merchandise Exports | |
Year	*Goods GNP*	*Amount*	*Percent Goods GNP*
1955	$ 214.5	$ 14.4	6.7%
1960	254.2	19.7	7.7
1965	338.4	26.5	7.8
1970	459.9	42.5	9.2
1975	694.0	107.1	15.4
1980	1,141.9	224.2	19.6
1981	1,289.2	234.3	18.3

Source: Goods GNP: "The National Income and Product Accounts of the
    United States, 1929–76" (U.S. Dept. of Commerce, 1981), p. 11
    and *Survey of Current Business,* July 1982, p. 24. *Merchandise Ex-
    ports: Economic Report of the President,* Feb. 1983, p. 276.

just corn and soy beans. Exports of manufactured
products as a percent of Goods GNP also roughly
doubled from 1970 to 1980 (from 6.4 percent to 12.6
percent).

Swings in our external trade have on occasion
been particularly large relative to short-term swings
in the level of general business activity. In the second
quarter of 1982, for example, real GNP was 1.6 percent below that for a year earlier—in 1972 prices a
decline from $1,502.2 billion to $1,478.4 billion, or
$23.8 billion. The decline in net exports (on a na-
tional accounts basis, and in 1972 prices) was $8.5
billion, an amount equal to 36 percent of the decline
in real GNP. If our external trade balance had not
weakened, the direct effect (before any multiplier)
would have been 500,000 more people employed.
With an allowance of about 2 for the multiplier effect,
the unemployment rate would have been a full percentage point lower.

Moreover, the stagnant state of the world economy, together with some quite specific trade problems (e.g., the problems of steel and autos), was forcing trade matters higher on the nation's political agenda. By 1981 our trade deficit with Japan was $16 billion and rising, and the major lump in this imbalance was automobiles. While the virtue of a multilateral trading system is precisely that trading patterns need not balance out bilaterally, bilateral imbalances that become large rapidly and are heavily focused on limited areas of domestic economy inevitably produce strong pressures for counter action.

Thus the 1980s have not been a propitious time for launching any great leap forward toward a more liberal international economic order. The problem for governments of the industrial world has been to retreat as little as possible from a comparatively open trading system, and to lay the bases for a resumption of economic expansion generally. This is obviously important for the industrial nations themselves, but it is of crucial importance to the middle- and lower-income countries. Except for sanctions incident to the Soviet gas pipeline, which did carry some potential for injecting further strains into the international economic and political order, the Administration has generally continued to strive for a liberal policy. It has resisted protectionist legislation, and it has urged a special fund for the IMF to deal with crises (something which could come into effect much more promptly than the cumbersome process of enlarging quotas). One might say, in short, that the Administration's instincts seem to have been aimed in the direction of a liberal international economic order, but neither has it articulated a fully developed international economic policy nor, until recently, did it organize itself well in this area.

While this is not the place to speculate about the Administration's future programs in international economic policy, it seems clear that the onrush of events will force actions in some key areas. First, the Administration must help the nation think through what its ''industrial policy'' is to be—what industries are to be encouraged or protected, and how, and what industries should be left to fade out. Moreover, even if our basic game plan is reliance on a liberal trading system, there will be some industries that we do not want to give up. There is, for example, a national security dimension to these issues, and they need a better intellectual ventilation, even though economists are understandably programmed to be suspicious when national security is invoked.

While it is easy to deplore whatever exchange-rate system happens to be operative at the moment, exchange-rate distortions and the disequilibrated trade patterns they have induced are themselves propelling us toward a disintegration of the liberal international economic order. Our policy posture must be one of more than ''Look, maw, no hands.'' Relative to exchange rates that would equilibrate trading patterns, the dollar has been seriously overvalued for some time. This was earlier assumed to be the result of our monetary policies and high interest rates, but after the decline in interest rates in 1982 the dollar strengthened further. Here is an urgent issue which international economic policy has yet to address.

Finally, the international financial system does need some tidying up. International financial collapses have occurred in history, they have usually produced severe economic dislocations (e.g., fifty years ago), and it is essential that our institutional arrangements be sufficiently strengthened to minimize this danger. Moreover, there is danger that our lending institutions, having extended too much credit too rapidly, may now overreact and force a further deterioration in the economies of middle- and lower-income nations.

In international economic policy the need is not so much for the Administration to change directions as for it to elevate the whole subject to a higher position on its active agenda. This clearly is beginning to occur.

Building Block IV

From the outset it was clear that supply-side economics was to play an important role in shaping the Administration's economic program. Here the Administration was focusing squarely on what history may well conclude was the domestic economy's most urgent need. That by the turn of the decade the economy seemed to have virtually no capability to deliver further gains in real incomes was evident from the data, which have been reviewed earlier in this lecture. Moreover, there was emerging a consensus about some things that needed to be done—e.g., major tax changes to encourage more rapid capital formation and to reduce the average age of technology in use. The need for this seemed clear, since the amount of capital (in real terms) per person in the labor force has increased little since the middle of the 1970s. This has been in sharp contrast to the 2.5 percent per year enlargement of capital per worker which had characterized our history.

Unfortunately this concern about a real problem metamorphosed into preoccupation with a highly vernacularized form of supply-side economics, and what should have been a major accomplishment has been a disappointment. This issue came into focus as an implementation of the Laffer Curve. Now admittedly there are not many routes to professional immortality for an economist, but there is one—namely to have a curve or a law bear one's name. Dr. Gresham succeeded with his dictum that bad money drives out good. Professor Phillips has his curve. And now Arthur Laffer may also have made it.

The trouble is that the sum total of the analytical literature establishing the case for the Laffer Curve is apparently an envelope on whose back has been drawn a curve first rising from zero revenue, with tax rates at zero, and then showing revenues declining again toward zero as tax rates get too high. What, however, are the parameters of the curve? At what level of tax rates does a further rate increase produce an absolute decline in revenues? Are we already in that zone? There have been no careful empirical analyses to answer these important questions. If important public policies are to be based, at least in part, on this concept, answers to these questions become important. For the Phillips Curve, Professor Phillips produced a long article carefully analyzing empirical evidence (which spawned extensive further work by others); there is no such analysis for the Laffer Curve. Only the envelope is available—together with anecdotal citations about cases where tax rates were reduced and revenues were larger the next year. (This would inevitably occur, even with no supply-side or fiscal-policy stimulus, so long as the revenue value of the tax rate reduction was less than the annual increment of revenues from ongoing economic growth.) There was really little but the assertion that with tax-rate reduction the economy would be so energized that we would have not only higher production and employment but such an outpouring of revenues that the deficit would be reduced also.

This is not, however, to denigrate supply-side concerns. Because there is never enough income and output to do everything we would like to do, economic policy and economists must be concerned about increasing the productivity of our economic resources. This has been a concern of economics at least ever since it emerged as a distinctive intellectual discipline. It is well for us to remember that the title of Adam Smith's book was not *The Wealth of Nations,* but *An Inquiry into the Nature and Causes of the Wealth of Nations.* That has a decidedly supply-side sound, and the book is largely concerned with enlarging the nation's wealth—or, as we would put it today, output and income in real terms. It is unfortunate that legitimate concerns about the need to revitalize the economy's capability to deliver gains in real incomes were given such a narrow focus.

Building Block V

The final building block in the President's economic program was a concern that government and the public sector were enlarging too rapidly. The concern was that this enlargement was contributing to the erosion of the economy's vitality and was in danger of going so far as to weaken the foundations of a liberal political order.

This expansion in the scope and reach of the public sector has characterized the entire industrial world. The rise in government spending from 1973 to 1980 absorbed (through taxation or government's preemptive borrowing) up to 78 percent of the rise in GNP for Sweden, and for five of the nine countries listed in Table 12 the figure exceeded 50 percent.

The figure for the U.S. was 34 percent, the lowest of the nine countries. For the United States, however, this incremental ratio was itself rising rapidly as we moved out of the 1970s. From 1979 to 1981, for example, the rise in government spending in the United States (federal, state, and local) was equal to 45 percent of the rise in GNP, or over 50 percent of the rise in net national product (which is a better measure of the pie to be divided). Moreover, the reach of government was expanding rapidly in the

Table 12. Increase in Government Spending as a Percent of the Increase in GNP, 1973–1980

Country	Percent
Belgium	65.3
Canada	43.1
France	51.6
Germany	54.9
Japan	37.4
Netherlands	74.3
Sweden	77.8
U.K.	46.3
U.S.	34.2

Source: Based on data in the Annual Report, Bank for International Settlements, Basel, Switzerland, June 1981, p. 24.

United States through the explosion of regulation.
And government can claim resources just as certainly
through such measures as regulatory mandates or
loan guarantees as through direct outlays in the
budget.

Now both logic and the empirical evidence suggest that this growing preemption of economic resources could be expected to have an adverse effect
on gains in output and real incomes. As the private
sector's share of the national income and output is
reduced, some part of this reduction will be at the
expense of capital outlays. While economic progress
involves far more than just an enlarging amount of
capital per worker, it is a fact that there has been a
rough correspondence between the rate of gain in
output per man-hour and the rate of growth in capital
per worker. Nor has the rise in the share of national
income preempted by the public sector been accounted for by a rise in public investment, which,
supplementing capital formation in the private sector,
might show undiminished increases in capital per
worker. In fact, public investment has been repre-
senting a declining share of government outlays.

The empirical data are at least consistent with
the hypothesis that a growing share of the national
income going to the public sector would have an
adverse effect on gains in productivity and real incomes. According to the Bank for International Settlements the change in the rate of growth from
1960–1973 to 1973–1981 for eleven industrial countries is inversely correlated with the change between
those periods in public sector spending as a percentage of the national income. While sluggish economic
conditions produce an enlargement of public outlays

(e.g., for income support), there is a growing conviction that causation also runs the other way.

> The growing burden of taxation and other levies on earnings saps initiative and the will to work and encourages the emergence of a parallel economy with all the distortions that this inevitably brings in its train. More generally, the rising share of the public sector gradually stifles the activity of the enterprise sector, while the justified aversion to large public sector deficits precludes the implementation of an anti-cyclical policy along traditional lines. [15]

While this would take us beyond the scope of our assigned subject, it is not amiss to point out that this growing proportion of the economy accounted for by the public sector does carry with it adverse implications also for a liberal political order. The control of government by the citizenry can metamorphose into a *de facto* control of people by government as their lives increasingly became managed by bureaucracies which are not really controlled by either the citizens or their elected representatives.

That the President has succeeded in nudging the budget toward a less rapid rate of expansion is clear enough from the data—and even clearer from the anguished cries of beneficiaries and their allied bureaucracies. Civilian spending increased about half as rapidly from 1981 to 1982 as during the three prior fiscal years. There are apt to be unintended casualties in any major restructuring of budget priorities, and history may well show that some programs this time were cut too severely. The fact is, however, that the time had clearly come for more severe budgeting of government outlays. We do now face the possibility that enough interest groups have a sufficient immediate stake in a continuing enlargement of civilian programs that the normal processes of government are virtually powerless to control them. Impeccable as the original objectives of programs have been, many have had unintended adverse side effects, and the cumulative effect of their preempting a growing proportion of the national income (here and in other economies) has contributed to a reduced capability to deliver gains in real income.[16] And gains in real after-tax incomes still clearly have a high priority for the citizenry generally (and nowhere does that seem to be more explicitly clear than for those earning their paychecks in our educational institutions).

And on Grading Economics

Before this midterm examination is concluded, it might be useful to ask ourselves what kind of a grade the managers of economic policy, here and in other industrial countries, would today give the discipline of economics and its practitioners. Hopefully it would be a passing grade, but it would almost certainly be well short of an "A." There would, I believe, be at least two sets of legitimate criticisms. First, after a half century of intellectual ferment about the matter, the theory of fiscal policy remains blurred, confused, in disarray. For one thing, what came to be the conventional compensatory-fiscal-policy wisdom did tend to jettison the fiscal-discipline dimension which the always-balanced-budget philosophy contributed to the expenditure process.

To the extent that the agenda for economic policy in one period is influenced by antecedent intellectual activity, what started out to be compensatory fiscal policy thus made its contribution to the rapid rise in the share of income and output absorbed by the public sector—a rate of rise which has become an increasingly troublesome problem for governments to handle today.

Moreover, the implications of the fact that larger deficits require more Treasury borrowing were tardily and inadequately developed. Thus, according to the old conventional fiscal-policy theory a tax reduction with a revenue value of, say, $20 billion would add to the GNP $20 billion times a multiplier (usually about 2). This, however, overlooked the fact that with less revenue the Treasury must then borrow more, and that increment of Treasury borrowing reduced the volume of funds available to other borrowers. The magnitide and even direction of the impact on economic activity from a tax reduction or increase in outlays, after an allowance for this financing effect, become less certain. Analytically the financial loop must be closed.

The extent of this intellectual diarray has been indicated in the Reagan years, during which not only political leaders but many economists have been urging tax increases, or a cancellation of earlier tax reductions, in order to reduce the deficit, in order to improve prospects for an expansion of employment and production. If Alvin Hansen (virtually the intellectual entrepreneur for fiscal-policy theory) has been listening "up there" to this national debate, he must have been invoking *The New Yorker's* department of "How's That Again?"

The managers of economic policy can also justifiably criticize economics for providing surprisingly little light about the optimum process or path for getting from here to there. The discipline continues to be essentially one of comparative statics. By the early 1980s the United States found itself with excessively high rates of both inflation and unemployment and negligible gains in real incomes. Our historical experience suggested that the economy could operate with lower rates of both and at the same time deliver strong gains in productivity and real incomes. The analytical underpinning of the Carter Administration's strategy, that the economy could attain lower rates of unemployment by accepting further increase in the rate of inflation, proved wrong. The analytical underpinning of the Reagan Administration's strategy, that we could get to lower rates of both inflation and unemployment with minimal trauma, also proved to be wrong. Both Presidents could reasonably insist that economic analysis gave them surprisingly little wisdom about the process of getting the economy to where they wanted it to be.

Concluding Observations

The time has now come to look back over the landscape through the tops of our bifocals to see if there are any general conclusions to be drawn. The task of evaluation is not an easy one. Ours is a government with a separation of powers among three coequal branches of government, plus some important agencies (e.g., the Federal Reserve) positioned uneasily among the three. The net performance of any one of the three is not easy to evaluate. Judgments about the proper objectives of national policy will differ, and there are no unambiguous criteria for "right" objectives and "wrong" objectives. Even so, the nation cannot escape asking if Reaganomics is a success or a failure, and that is the question posed here. The answer, of course, is "Both." There are some items on the minus side and some on the plus side. These judgments must, of course, be tentative, since economic policies and processes work themselves out over a long period of time. Policies which produce good near-term results may be building problems for the future, and policies which seem to be losers in the short term may be establishing the foundation for a better economic performance for the long pull. With less than two years of Reaganomics, that well-publicized laureate grade of "Incomplete" is inevitable, but it is also of limited value.[17] Even if the end of the journey is not in sight, we must still ask ourselves if we are on the right road.

In all probability history will record that the most serious shortfall of the Administration's economic program was in the interrelated matter of budget policy and its interpretation of supply-side economics. At a time when the high-employment budget was only roughly in balance, though moving toward a projected high-employment surplus in the $35 billion zone, a major three-installment tax reduction was proposed and passed.[18] The theoretical underpinning for the proposal (by a President who believed in a balanced budget) was, of course, twofold. Having less money in the till was a good way to discipline spending. And reduced tax rates would so sharpen incentives that more income would be earned and output produced. In addition to a stronger economy, therefore, the budget situation would also be improved by the enlarged revenues from the stronger economy.

The first rationale was probably right. Prospective deficits did force a slowing down in the rate of federal civilian spending, which rose 8.7 percent from FY 1981 to FY 1982—compared with 12.9 percent for the prior year and 13.3 percent per year from 1977 to 1980. The deficit, however, almost doubled, rising from $60 billion in FY 1981 to $111 billion last year. There were two reasons. Fiscal discipline could not be effective enough on civilian outlays to offset the $28 billion rise in defense spending. And the variant of supply-side economics which constituted the second rationale for the tax reduction did not deliver. While roughly half of the prospective deficit for FY 1983 would be accounted for by the weak economy, that would still leave a high-employment deficit in the $75 billion zone. And there is now danger that the failure of this popularized or vernacularized supply-side theory, which never had a strong theoretical and empirical foundation, may erode support for some changes in policy needed to strengthen the basic capability of the economy. Indeed, the bipartisan support that emerged in 1980 for some basic actions seems to be fading.

There are, however, some major entries on the plus side. Reaganomics has made a contribution to steadier monetary policy, and the President has generally supported the Federal Reserve in its needed but thankless efforts to restabilize the economy. The need for stronger fiscal discipline on the outlay side has been moved higher on the national agenda, and this has been needed (regardless of one's preferred pattern of federal outlays). The Administration, after some detours, is now also in a position to give some leadership to arresting, or at least retarding, forces propelling the world away from a liberal economic order.

Finally, Reaganomics broadly defined has delivered dramatic progress in regaining control of the price level. The acceleration in the rate of inflation to double-digit levels by 1980 was producing such profound economic and social displacement effects as to raise questions about the survival of our liberal institutions. The rate of inflation has been brought down to the 5 to 6 percent zone, and more quickly than had been anticipated. And underlying trends in productivity, wage changes, and labor costs per unit of output suggest that this improvement can be more than transitory.

The most severe criticism of this exercise in disinflation is the high rate of unemployment. The Administration was itself overly sanguine about the extent to which there could be disinflation with minimal adverse effects on employment. In fact, the momentum from multiyear wage contracts, price-level escalators that overadjusted, repeated broken promises of government to deal with inflation, and the pervasive inflation-mindedness—these all made inevitable a painful confrontation with disinflationary policies. An economic milieu had to be created in which markets would not accept price increases and the inflationary wage increases that had become habitual could not be extracted. There had to be created, in short, economic conditions in which inflationary prices would mean lost sales and inflationary wages would mean lost jobs. It was failure to face this interim of adjustment that led us to accelerating inflation during the latter half of the last decade—and which has caused the adjustment to be so severe.

Does this mean that the lower rate of inflation will prevail only if high rates of unemployment continue? I do not believe so. The rational expectations theory of the winding-down process implied, or led the Administration to suggest, that it would all be fairly painless. It was wrong about the ease of the unwinding process but right about the fundamental end result—that on an ongoing basis lower rates of inflation do not mean lower employment, and willingness to accept successively higher rates of inflation will not sustain higher employment.

Notes

1. Annual Report, Council of Economic Advisers, January 1969, p. 123.
2. *Towards Full Employment and Price Stability* (Paris: OECD, 1977), p. 39.
3. *Economic Outlook* (Paris: OECD, July 1982), pp. 14–15.
4. *Economic Outlook* (Paris: OECD, July 1973), pp. 43, 103.
5. Data are from *International Financial Statistics Yearbook, 1982* (Washington, D.C.: International Monetary Fund), pp. 62–65.
6. For a quick review of the concept's genealogy, cf. Edmund S. Phelps, *Inflation Policy and Unemployment Theory* (New York: Norton, 1972), pp. 41–57.

7. Milton Friedman, "The Role of Monetary Policy." *American Economic Review,* vol. 58, no. 1, March 1968, p. 8.

8. For a careful, scholarly exposition of these interrelationships, cf. Robert J. Gordon, "Output Fluctuations and Gradual Price Adjustment." *Journal of Economic Literature,* June 1981, pp. 493–530.

9. *America's New Beginning: A Program for Economic Recovery* (White House, February 19, 1981), p. 24.

10. *Blue Chip Economic Indicators* (Arlington, Va.: Eggert Economic Enterprises Capital Publications, February 19, 1981), p. 31.

11. *America's New Beginning: A Program for Economic Recovery,* p. 24.

12. Annual Report, Council of Economic Advisers, February 1982, p. 76.

13. Cf. John P. Judd and John L. Scadding, "The Search for a Stable Money Demand Function." *Journal of Economic Literature,* September 1982, pp. 993–1023. This article contains an excellent bibliography of the literature on the subject. Also Barbara A. Bennett, " 'Shift Adjustments' to the Monetary Aggregates." *Economic Review,* Federal Reserve Bank of San Francisco, Spring 1982, pp. 6–18.

14. Cf. *The Economic & Budget Outlook: An Update* (Congressional Budget Office, September 1, 1982), pp. 79–85. Also "Monetary Policy Report to the Congress." *Federal Reserve Bulletin,* August 1982, pp. 443–452.

15. Annual Report, Bank for International Settlements, Basel, Switzerland, 1982, p. 3.

16. Cf. Roger A. Freeman, *The Wayward Welfare State* (Stanford, Calif.: Hoover, 1981).
17. The grade suggested by George Stigler, who had just received the Nobel Prize for Economiics.
18. *Survey of Current Business,* August 1981, p. 6.